WISE SAYINGS

of

ST

FRANCIS

WISE SAYINGS

of

ST

FRANCIS

LION

Compiled by Andrea Skevington
This edition copyright © 2012 Lion
Hudson

The author asserts the moral right
to be identified as the author of this
work

A Lion Book
an imprint of
Lion Hudson plc
Wilkinson House, Jordan Hill Road,
Oxford OX2 8DR, England
www.lionhudson.com
ISBN 978 0 7459 5564 3

Distributed by:
UK: Marston Book Services, PO Box
269, Abingdon, Oxon, OX14 4YN
USA: Trafalgar Square Publishing, 814
N. Franklin Street, Chicago, IL 60610
USA Christian Market: Kregel
Publications, PO Box 2607, Grand
Rapids, Michigan 49501

First edition 2012
10 9 8 7 6 5 4 3 2 1 0

Typeset in 11.5/12 Perpetua and
10/24 Zapfino

Printed and bound in China

ACKNOWLEDGMENTS

BACKGROUNDS

iStock: Jussi Santaniemi

ILLUMINATED MANUSCRIPTS

Corbis: Fine Art Photographic Library

MOTIFS

iStock: Jamie Farrant, alexpixel,
Bodhi Hill, andipantz, vahlakova, Diane
Labombarbe, feoris

PHOTOGRAPHS

Corbis: pp. 17, 18–19 Ocean;
p. 43 The Gallery Collection;
pp. 48–49 Elio Ciol

iStock: pp. 6–7 Jowita Stachowiak;
pp. 8–9 Massimo Merlini; pp. 14–15
Kostyantyn Ivanyshen; pp. 22–23
brytta; p. 29 Iraida Bassi; pp. 30–31
Pawel Gaul; p. 36 Frank van den Bergh;
pp. 40–41, 50–51 Amarphoto;
pp. 52–53 Giorgio Fochesato;
pp. 54–55 seraficus; pp. 58–59
Ivonne Wierink-van Wetten

COVER

Background: Jussi Santaniemi/iStock

Illuminated manuscript:
The Gallery Collection/Corbis

Photograph: Duncan Walker/iStock

ONTENTS

INTRODUCTION

The life and teachings of St Francis have
inspired many through the ages, and have much
wisdom for our lives today. St Francis reminds
us to be peacemakers, to love and respect all
people and all creatures.

This book draws from the full range of
St Francis' writings: there are prayers and
meditations, stories from his life, and rules he
lay down for his communities. His words are
full of love and devotion, and show the power
of gentleness.

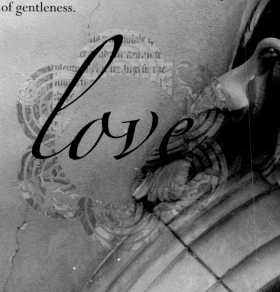

love

In the beginning,

GOD

Lord God: you alone are holy,
you who work wonders! You are strong, you are great,
you are the Most High,
you are the almighty King,
you, holy Father, King of heaven and earth.

Lord God: you are Three and you are One,
you are goodness, all goodness,
you are the highest Good,
Lord God, living and true.

Amen

FROM THE EXHORTATION TO THE PRAISES OF GOD

God,
all powerful, most holy
sublime ruler of all, you alone are good –
supremely, fully, completely good,
may we render to you all praise,
all honour and all blessing:
may we always ascribe to you alone
everything that is good!

Amen

PRAISE FOR ALL HOURS

How glorious it is to have
so holy and great a Father
in Heaven.

**PROLOGUE TO THE FIRST LETTER TO THE
FAITHFUL PENITENTS**

My God and my all.

**MEDITATION PRAYER FROM
FRANCISCANS PROVINCE OF ENGLAND**

We give you thanks because,
as you created us through your Son,
so by the holy love
with which you loved us
you willed your Son to be born
true God and true man
of the glorious and holy Virgin Mary,
and through his cross and blood and death
it was your will to set us free
from our captivity.

PRAISE AND THANKSGIVING

Most high, glorious God,
enlighten the darkness
of my heart and give me Lord,
a correct faith, a certain hope,
a perfect charity, sense and knowledge,
so that I may carry out
Your holy and true command.

Amen

PRAYER BEFORE A CRUCIFIX

We adore you, Lord Jesus Christ,
in all the churches
throughout the world,
and we bless you,
because by your holy Cross
you have redeemed the world.
Amen

FROM THE TESTAMENT OF ST FRANCIS

I beg you, Lord,
let the fiery, gentle power
of your love
take possession of my soul,
and snatch it away
from everything under heaven,
that I may die
for love of your love
as you saw fit to die
for love of mine.

PRAYER OF SELF GIVING

soul

THE LORD'S

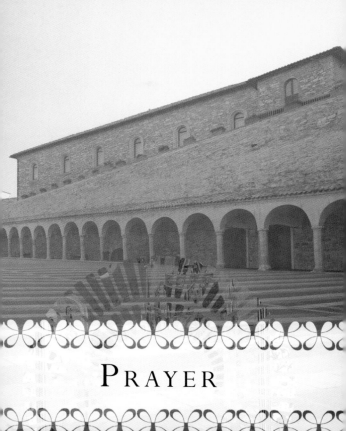

PRAYER

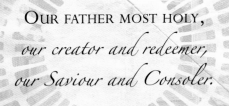

OUR FATHER MOST HOLY,
our creator and redeemer,
our Saviour and Consoler.

WHO ARE IN HEAVEN,
in the angels and saints
enlightening them that they
may know, for you, Lord,
are love, dwelling in them and filling
them with your divinity, that bliss
may be theirs, for you, Lord, are the
highest Good, the eternal Good,
from whom all goodness flows,
without whom nothing is good.

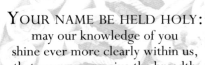

YOUR NAME BE HELD HOLY:
may our knowledge of you
shine ever more clearly within us,
that we may perceive the breadth
of your blessings, the extent of your
promises, the height of your majesty,
the depth of your judgements.

holy

YOUR KINGDOM COME:
rule us now, through grace,
and bring us at last to your
kingdom of light where we
shall see you as you are,
and our love for you
will be made perfect,
our union blissful,
our joy unending, in you.

YOUR WILL BE DONE ON
EARTH AS IN HEAVEN
may we love you
with all our heart,
ever thinking of you;
with all our soul,
ever longing for you;
with all our mind,
directing all our aims to you
and seeking nothing but your glory;
with all our strength,
spending all our energies
and all our senses of soul and body
to serve only your love and nothing else.

May we love our neighbours as ourselves;
drawing them all to your love
in so far as we can,
sharing their good fortune
as if it were our own,
helping them to bear their trials
and doing them no wrong.

GIVE US THIS DAY OUR
DAILY BREAD:

your beloved Son
our Lord Jesus Christ,
that we may remember,
understand and revere
the love he showed for us,
and all he said and did
and suffered for our sake.

FORGIVE US OUR SINS
through your mercy beyond words,
through the power of the passion
of your beloved Son,
through the merits and intercession
of the Virgin Mary
and of all your chosen ones.

AS WE FORGIVE THOSE WHO
SIN AGAINST US
and that we ourselves
cannot fully forgive,
make us fully forgive;
make us love our enemies,
truly, for your sake;
teach us how to pray sincerely
to you on their behalf;
and not to render harm for harm
to anyone, but rather try
to do good to all, in you!

AND LEAD US NOT INTO TEMPTATION
whether veiled or visible,
sudden or searing and prolonged.

BUT DELIVER US FROM EVIL
past, present and to come.
Amen

lead us

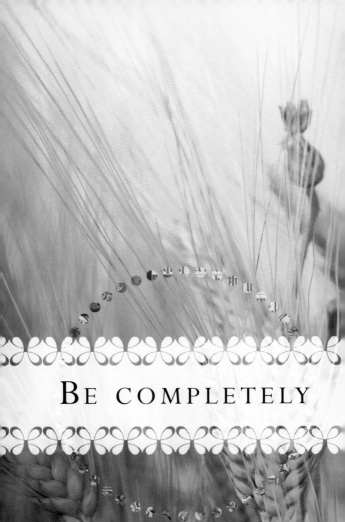

BE COMPLETELY

HUMBLE & GENTLE

Lord God;

You are love and charity, you are wisdom,
you are humility, you are patience,
you are beauty, you are sweetness,
you are safety, you are rest, you are joy,
you are our hope
and our delight,
you are justice, you are moderation
you are all our wealth
and riches overflowing.

FROM THE EXHORTATION

Let all the brothers strive to follow the humility and poverty of our Lord Jesus Christ and let them remember that we should have nothing else in the whole world except, as the Apostle says:

If we have food and clothing, we will be content with these.

They must rejoice when they live among people considered of little value and looked down upon, among the poor and the powerless, the sick and the lepers, and the beggars by the wayside.

When it is necessary, they may go for alms. Let them not be ashamed.

PRIMITIVE FIRST RULE

And we were simple and subject to all.

FROM THE TESTAMENT OF ST FRANCIS

Let all the brothers not have power or control especially among themselves; for, as the Lord says in the Gospel: *the rulers of the Gentiles lord it over them, and their great ones are tyrants over them. It will not be so among the brothers. Whoever wishes to be great among them must be their minister and servant. Whoever wishes to be first among them must be their slave.* Let no one be called "prior", but let everyone in general be called a lesser brother. Let one wash the feet of the other.

PRIMITIVE FIRST RULE

If anyone, wishing by divine inspiration to accept this life, comes to our brothers, let him be received by them with kindness.

Let him sell all his belongings and be conscientious in giving everything to the poor.

Let all the brothers wear poor clothes and, with the blessing of God, they can patch them with sackcloth and other pieces, for our Lord says in the Gospel: *Those who put on fine clothing and live in luxury are in royal palaces.*

In accordance with the Gospel, it may be lawful for them to eat of all the food that is placed before them.

PRIMITIVE FIRST RULE

Let the brothers who know
how to work do so and exercise
that trade they have learned,
provided it is not contrary to
the good of their souls and
can be performed honestly.
And for their work they can
receive whatever is necessary
excepting money. And when
it is necessary, they may seek
alms like other poor people.

PRIMITIVE FIRST RULE

I Brother Francis send wishes of
health to Brother Anthony, my bishop.
It pleases me that you teach sacred
theology to the brothers, as long as
in the words of the Rule you "do not
extinguish the Spirit of prayer and
devotion" with study of this kind.

LETTER TO ST ANTHONY

devotion

All who love the Lord with their whole heart, their whole soul and mind, and with their strength, and love their neighbour as themselves, and who despise the tendency in their humanity to sin, receive the Body and Blood of our Lord Jesus Christ and bring forth from within themselves fruits worthy of true penance.

PROLOGUE TO THE FIRST RULE

38

When the brothers go through
the world, let them take nothing
for the journey, no staff, nor
bag, nor bread, nor money.
Whatever house they enter, let
them first say "Peace to this
house!" They may eat and drink
whatever is provided for as long
as they remain in that house.
Take nothing for the journey.

PRIMITIVE FIRST RULE (ADAPTED)

BLESSED ARE

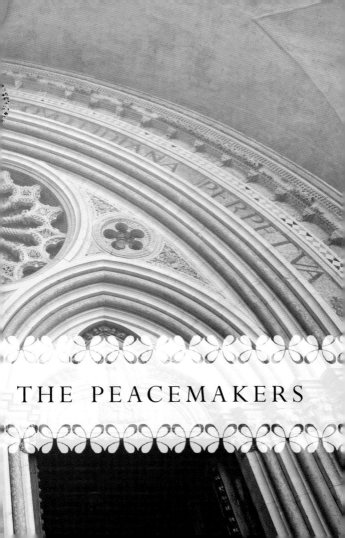

THE PEACEMAKERS

Lord, make me an instrument of your peace

Where there is hatred,
Let me sow love;
Where there is injury, pardon;
Where there is doubt, faith;
Where there is despair, hope;
Where there is darkness, light;
And where there is sadness, Joy.

O Divine Master grant that I may
Not so much seek to be consoled
As to console;
To be understood,
As to understand;
To be loved as to love.
For it is in giving that we receive,
It is in pardoning that we are
pardoned.
And it is in dying that we are
Born to eternal life.
Amen.

THE PEACE PRAYER

sow love

Lord God:
You are beauty,
you are gentleness,
you are our shelter,
our guard
and our defender,

you are strength, you are refreshment,
you are our hope.
you are our faith.
you are our love,
you are our complete consolation,
you are our life everlasting,
great and wonderful Lord,
all powerful God, merciful Saviour!

FROM THE EXHORTATION

Let all the brothers be careful not to slander or engage in disputes; let them strive, instead, to keep silence whenever God gives them the grace. Let them not quarrel among themselves or with others but strive to respond humbly, saying: *We are worthless slaves*.

Let them love one another, as the Lord says: *This is my commandment, that you love one another as I have loved you*.

Let them *not resist an evildoer. But if anyone strikes* them *on the right cheek,* let them *turn the other also. If anyone wants to take* their *coat,* let them *give* their *cloak as well*. Let them *give to everyone who begs from* them; *and if anyone takes away* their *goods,* let them *not ask for them again*.

Wherever they may be, let all my brothers remember that they have given themselves and abandoned their bodies to the Lord Jesus Christ. For love of him they must make themselves vulnerable to their enemies, both visible and invisible, because the Lord says: *Those who want to save their life will lose it, and those who lose their life for my sake will save it in eternal life*.

PRIMITIVE FIRST RULE

And now, brother, listen to the conclusion. Above all the graces and all the gifts of the Holy Spirit which Christ grants to his friends, is the grace of overcoming oneself, and accepting willingly, out of love for Christ, all suffering, injury, discomfort and contempt.

LITTLE FLOWERS

One day at St Mary, St Francis called Brother Leo and said: "Brother Leo, write this down."

He answered: "I'm ready."

"Write what true joy is," he said. "A messenger comes and says that all the masters of theology in Paris have joined the Order — write: that is not true joy. Or all the prelates beyond the mountain — archbishops and bishops, or the King of France and the King of England — write: that is not true joy. Or that my friars have gone to the unbelievers and have converted all of them to the faith; or that I have so much grace from God that I heal the sick and I perform many miracles. I tell you that true joy is not in all those things."

"But what is true joy?"

"I am returning from Perugia and I am coming here at night, in the dark. It is winter time and wet and muddy and so cold that icicles form at the edges of my habit and keep striking my legs, and blood flows from such wounds. And I come to the gate, all covered with mud and cold and ice, and after I have knocked and called for a long time, a friar comes and asks: 'Who are you?' I answer: 'Brother Francis.' And he says 'Go away. This is not a decent time to be going about. You can't come in.'

"And when I insist again, he replies: 'Go away. You are a simple and uneducated fellow. From now on don't stay with us any more. We are so many and so important that we don't need you.'

"But I still stand at the gate and say: 'For the love of God, let me come in tonight.' And he answers: 'I won't. Go to the Crosiers' Place and ask there.'

"I tell you that if I kept patience and was not upset – that is true joy and true virtue and the salvation of the soul."

LITTLE FLOWERS

salvation

Praised be You, my Lord,

through those who give pardon
    for Your love,
and bear infirmity and tribulation.

Blessed are those who endure
in peace for by You,
Most High,
they shall be crowned.

FROM THE CANTICLE OF THE SUN

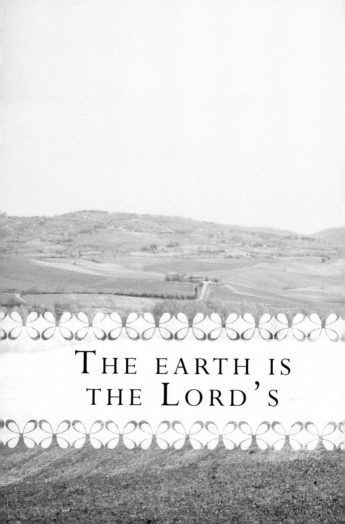

THE EARTH IS
THE LORD'S

AND EVERYTHING
IN IT

God, all powerful, most holy,
most high and supreme;
Father: holy and righteous;
Lord: king of heaven and earth;
we thank you for yourself,
because by your holy will
and through your only Son
and the Holy Spirit
you created all things,
spiritual and material.
You made us in your
image and likeness
and placed us in paradise.

PRAISE AND THANKSGIVING

And as he went on his way, with great fervour, St Francis lifted up his eyes, and saw on some trees by the wayside a great multitude of birds; and being much surprised, he said to his companions, "Wait for me here by the way, whilst I go and preach to my little sisters the birds"; and entering into the field, he began to preach to the birds which were on the ground, and suddenly all those also on the trees came round him, and all listened while St Francis preached to them, and did not fly away until he had given them his blessing.

LITTLE FLOWERS

Most High, all powerful, good Lord,
Yours are the praises, the glory, the honour,
and all blessing.

To You alone, Most High, do they belong,
and no man is worthy to mention Your name.

Be praised, my Lord, through all your creatures,
especially through my lord Brother Sun,
who brings the day; and you give light through him.
And he is beautiful and radiant in all his splendour!
Of you, Most High, he bears the likeness.

Praise be You, my Lord, through Sister Moon
and the stars, in heaven you formed them
clear and precious and beautiful.

Praised be You, my Lord, through Brother Wind,
and through the air, cloudy and serene,
and every kind of weather through which
You give sustenance to Your creatures.

Praised be You, my Lord, through Sister Water,
which is very useful and humble and precious and chaste.

Praised be You, my Lord, through Brother Fire,
through whom you light the night and he is beautiful
and playful and robust and strong.

Praised be You, my Lord, through Sister Mother Earth,
who sustains us and governs us and who produces
varied fruits with coloured flowers and herbs.

Praise and bless my Lord,
and give Him thanks
and serve Him with great humility.

Amen

CANTICLE OF THE SUN

Whoever shall observe these things
may he be filled in heaven
with the blessing of the most high Father,
and may he be filled on earth
with the blessing of his beloved son,
together with the Holy Spirit, the Consoler,
and all the powers of heaven and all the saints.
And I, brother Francis, your worthless servant,
as far as I am able, approve this most
holy blessing both internally and externally.

Amen

Blessing of St Francis

blessing

BIBLIOGRAPHY

Z. El Bey, *The Complete Writings of St. Francis of Assisi*, Seattle: Createspace, 2009.

Friar Kajetan Essar, O.F.M, *The Writings of St. Francis of Assisi*, Italy: The Franciscan Archive, 1999.

WEBSITES:

www.tssf.org.uk – Franciscan Friars Third Order

www.franciscans.ie – Irish Franciscans

www.franciscanfriarstor.com – Franciscan Friars, TOR

www.friar.org – Franciscans Province of England